MW00897951

RADIOLOGY JOURNAL

THIS JOURNAL BELONGS TO:

THE RAD LOOK

92941459R00062

Made in the USA
San Bernardino, CA
05 November 2018